Magnetic North
Current Installation Photography in Finland

Edited by
Caryn Faure Walker

UNIVERSITY OF ART AND DESIGN
HELSINKI UIAH

The Finnish Museum of Photography

Helsinki

Magnetic North: Current Installation Photography in Finland
Book edited by Caryn Faure Walker

Published by
University of Art and Design Helsinki UIAH
The Finnish Museum of Photography

Publication Series of University of Art and Design
Helsinki UIAH, B 67
ISBN 951-558-084-6
ISSN 0782-1778

Publication Series of The Finnish Museum of Photography, 13
ISSN 1239-6141

Photographs © 2001
Elina Brotherus, Marjaana Kella, Ola Kolehmainen, The Estate
of Andrei Lajunen, Jyrki Parantainen

Essay © 2001
Caryn Faure Walker, Mika Hannula

The following organizations and institutions have supported
the publication of this book:

University of Art and Design Helsinki UIAH
The Finnish Museum of Photography
Frame, Finnish Fund for Art Exchange
The Ministry of Foreign Affairs Finland
The New Art Gallery Walsall
Papyrus Finland Oy

Associate editors: Jane Becker and Susan Butler

Graphic design: Jorma Hinkka, Graafiset Neliöt Oy, Helsinki

Colour separations: Repromestarit Oy, Helsinki

Paper: Papyrus Finland Oy, LumiSilk 170 gsm

Printed by Erweko Painotuote Oy, Helsinki, 2001

Magnetic North: Current Installation Photography in Finland
Exhibition curated by Caryn Faure Walker
The New Art Gallery Walsall
September 28 to November 18, 2001

The following organizations and institutions have supported
the production of new commissioned works and the
exhibition:

University of Art and Design Helsinki UIAH
The Finnish Cultural Foundation
The Ministry of Foreign Affairs Finland
The Embassy of Finland, London
The Finnish Institute in London
hasan and partners
The New Art Gallery Walsall
Visiting Arts Unit

Caryn Faure Walker is an American writer and curator who
lives in London. A founder of the art magazine *Artscribe*,
she has also been editor of *MAKE, The Magazine of
Womens'Art*. She has curated exhibitions of current art in
Great Britain, Continental Europe, the United States and
Finland.

Mika Hannula has a Ph.D. in political science. He is Reviews
Editor of *NU: the Nordic Art Review*, and the Director of
Helsinki Academy of Fine Arts.

Acknowledgements
The curators and artists of *Magnetic North* would like to thank
the following individuals and institutions for their assistance
with the exhibition and book:

Paulina Ahokas
Magnus Åklundh
Ilona Anhava
The Arts Council of Finland
Jane Becker
Susan Butler
Marianna Collander
Anna Copp
Joakim Eskildsen
Kirsi Gimishanov
Solenne Guillier & :gbagency, Paris
Mika Hannula
Ami Hasan, hasan & partners
Erna and Victor Hasselblad Foundation
Elina Heikka
Jorma Hinkka
Peter Jenkinson
Ulla Jokisalo
Edda Jonsdottir
Ari Kaivola
Jarmo Kauppinen
Timo Kelaranta
Kari Kenetti
Kristiina Kella
Neil Kent
Tiina Knuutila
Riitta Koskivirta
Pentti Kouri
Sari and Harri Laatio
Erkki and Ritva Lajunen
Torvald Lindberg
Anna-Maria Liukko

Olivier Loudin
Sami Luukkanen
Asko Mäkelä
Emily Marsden
Jukka Merta
Christer Nuutinen
Sirpa Päivinen
Elmeri Parantainen
Ritva Palander
Nina Pehkonen
Timothy Persons
Jukka Pietikäinen
David Pratley
Jorma Puranen
Antti Rimaaja
Deborah Robinson
Pirkko Salmela
Leena Saraste
Raimo Selenius
Marketta Seppälä
Marja Siiropää
Pirkko Siitari
Yrjö Sotamaa
Bengt Ståhle
Irma Swahn
Marja Söderlund
Marja-Terttu Kivirinta
Marjatta Tikkanen
Pekka Ylönen
Zink Gallery, Andy Milliken
and Ben Loveless

The photographers presented in this book have all studied in the UIAH Department of Photography. It is the only university level institution in Finland that provides training in photographic art. For close to 30 years now, the Department has been working consistently towards reinforcing the foundations of Finnish photography. The results have received growing international and national recognition in the past several years. The Finnish Ministry of Education has already twice given the highest rating to the Department by nominating it as a unit of excellence in artistic production.

Training at the UIAH Department of Photography emphasises the development of personal idiom and content. In the midst of the contemporary visual commotion and flood of images, we still need authors who have something personal to say, and the courage and skill to say it with photographs.

According to a Chinese proverb, only the surface of still water can reflect the star. Perhaps photography, withdrawn to its own silence – in the midsts of the current clamorous visual culture – offers a surface on which we may glimpse a fleeting reflection of meaning. This quotation noted by Professor Merja Salo, Dean of the UIAH Department of Photography, illustrates well the philosophy of current young photographers.

UIAH's mission is to cultivate visual intelligence in all areas of the visual and material cultures. Its graduates, Tapio Wirkkala, Timo Sarpaneva, Antti and Vuokko Nurmesniemi, Kaj Frack, Yrjö Kukkapuro, Stefan Lindfors, Jorma Puranen, Ilkka Suppanen, Harri Koskinen and many others have had a major impact on the development of contemporary design. The presentation of young Finnish photographers at The New Art Gallery Walsall highlights the celebration of the 130th anniversary of UIAH.

The UIAH is grateful to Caryn Faure Walker for her excellent work in curating the *Magnetic North* exhibition and editing this book. It catches the essence of contemporary Finnish photography. Jorma Hinkka has designed the book with great skill. I also want to express my warm thanks to Timothy Persons, who has helped us immensely in making new Finnish photography visible in the world.

Professor Yrjö Sotamaa
Rector of the University of Art and Design Helsinki UIAH

The Look of Love
The Phenomena of Urbanization in 1990s Helsinki

Mika Hannula

When talking about time, any kind of a period of time, one has to give in and admit rather soon that it is a difficult subject. Or as Tom Waits stated in the film *Rumblefish*, "time is a peculiar thing". It seems to disappear, but stay present. So far and simultaneously so near. When considering the place-related time of a city called Helsinki, it seems that the most fruitful way to approach the theme and its nuances is through a door opened by an anecdote.

It is stolen from a song by a band called *Ultra Bra*, a fine example of the spirit of 90s Helsinki. In the song, the group flirting with Finnish anti-imperialist protest schlagers, refers to the actual time in Helsinki, and compares it to near-by time zones. The result is that during the 90s, special Helsinki time no longer was one hour ahead (of Stockholm) or one hour behind (Moscow). It had finally reached a point where it was able to focus and enjoy its own time. Right here, right now.

A fairly important question emerges. What do the various artists and photographs shown in this exhibition have to do with this special Helsinki time, and in broader perspective, with the phenomena of urbanization of Helsinki in the 1990s? Well, in fact, everything and nothing. The larger frame can determine nothing of what happens on the micro level in the activities of any artist. It is personal time, personal experience and expectations, which are nevertheless connected to a larger frame – the frame that I will concentrate on. And in relation to this chosen focus, the answer is Helsinki time had everything to do with it because so much did change during the 90s that it could not have but enormously affected anyone connected to that location as they were in the midst of a major wake-up call.

What did then change so dramatically? As you might guess, just about everything, even if the cruelty is that so much remained the same. I will try to describe this by dealing with the interconnected themes of urbanization and the concept of Finnishness, that is, what kind of relationship do we thirty-somethings have to Finland?

But first to urbanization, which sounds a grand and serious subject, but is not. I am not referring to urbanization in any kind of strict sociological sense but as first-hand lived experience. And the best way to get closer to this experience is – surprise, surprise – to go for a drink. This, on purpose, is a mighty banal example, but an example that has consequences beyond anyone's imagination. I remember it all too well. Finland of the 80s was an Albania of the North: self-possessed and insular to the extreme, regulated by the heavy social democratic hand of the government. This control had a great deal to say about how Finns spent their free time, and how they tried to get where they wanted to go: oblivion with alcohol.

It is an historical fact. Until the year 1990 licensing laws in the whole of Finland were very strict. Getting a new license was almost impossible, and the pubs could stay open only until 10 p.m. Fancier restaurants and discos had the magical last serve hour at 12.30 a.m. I do not care to acknowledge how many dark nights I have frozen waiting outside these few joints, finding the only helping hand in the vodka flask that you had to carry with you in order to survive.

But then something happened. In the great summer of love of 1990, young, often inexperienced, entrepreneurs were given the right to sell, not alcohol or wine, but beer. At first, the opening hours were stretched to midnight, which, along with the fact of new bars and pubs coming up, caused a revolution. Then not that long after, the opening hours were extended to 2 a.m. Today, the choice is yours from hard liquor to fancier wines and the opening hours vary from between 2 a.m. and 4 a.m., hours reserved for places which no longer call themselves discotheques, but clubs.

But why was this so incredibly important? All those vast changes were, in fact, linked by fresh possibilities to be together and to spent time together – not to mention to make and to throw away money. In the early 90s, Finland was, to put it plainly, in a huge political mess. The country was in the midst of a horrifying identity crisis. How Finland stood was not how it had created itself after the war. Bye, bye badman, bye, bye Soviet Union, bye, bye. In relation to the economy, the disappearance of the Communist bloc was even more disastrous. Numbers, like diamonds, are man's best friend. When in 1991, almost half of Finnish exports were to the Soviet Union, the export market to the USSR collapsed drastically in 1992. What did not drop was the level of unemployment, which skyrocketed from 4% to 5% to more that 20% during 1993–1994. For a short period, Finland was number one on the list of countries with the highest unemployment in Europe.

To add to its difficulties, Finland decided to join the European Union, becoming a member in the beginning of 1995. And this brings me to the cultural implications of this turmoil, which are not at all so destructive or negative. On the contrary, they served the needs of the new generation, which no longer wanted to accept the story of Finland as a monolithic, homogenous nation-state where only one 'proper' opinion in each field of enquiry in Finnish society was accepted as correct. In other words, the crises I spoke about above gave space on the floor to the very varied views and opinions, which, for the first time, made Helsinki (in lesser terms than cities like Turku and Tampere) an urbanized environment. Somewhere which bred, supported and renewed itself.

The Look of Love

All of a sudden there were a plurality of voices, a plurality of alternatives for shopping, eating and drinking out. A plurality which did not ask permission to be loudly visible, but did it anyhow. There were a plurality of radio stations, new political parties, (a lot of illegal party parties) that sprang from the miseries of the 80s; these now got their real chance. If in the 80s the Establishment was still controlling almost everything, in the early 90s its credibility was in shambles. It was not asking the right questions, not to mention being able to give any valid answers for the challenges and demands of the radically altered situation in Finland.

So my claim is, based on my experience, that this newly found plurality was celebrated and propped up in the bars and clubs during the early 90s. It was all very exciting, extravagant and confusing. If the larger scale future perspectives were dead, that did not matter. It was a rare kind of a moment when you felt a sudden rush to do whatever you wanted to do – no matter if that something had a market or other kinds of support. And in-between you went to the bar and got, well, you know, happily drunk.

At this stage, I think it is necessary to stop – for a minute. Of course, I am painting a picture of the early 90s, which is extremely rosy and sentimental. It was particularly *my* time, and I was there. Standing as the doorman, serving behind the bar, hustling behind the 'decs,' sleeping under the tables. Besides these nightlife activities, I contributed to a lot of Finnish magazines and newspapers, writing essays and reviews, commenting feverishly on anything between international politics and the local house music scene. My motivation was very simple: a great need to participate in many different ways and in various fields of the society.

But I was not only there. Actually, most of the time I was not living in Finland, but studying for my Ph.D. in political science in Berlin. At the same time, I visited and worked a great deal in Helsinki. I had left the country, as soon it was possible, because, for reasons I could articulate only later, I was appalled at the necessity to be like everyone else and appalled at the discouragement of individuality. The problem of openly expressed individuality was not only apparent in the hard core areas of religious choice or sexual preferences. In the early 80s all you needed to have was the wrong kind of T-shirt to be singled out and criticised for trying to be special and somehow better. (In fact, in my case it was a *Bob Marley* shirt. Friends of mine had similar troubles with *The Jam* and *The Police* shirts). It sounds strange, but I believe I am not alone in claiming that Finland was a country where it was a sign of outrageously bad taste to enjoy openly what you did – whatever it was that you did. When the colour of reality is grey on grey, smiling was a sin.

However, this country, which for me and for very many others who had moved abroad, became – referring to Salman Rushdie's famous concept – an imagined homeland; one partly idealised and strongly constructed. For us this changed rapidly in the 90s. That suffocated self-importance and hysterical fear of otherness had not disappeared, but it had significantly eased off. When I asked friends of mine how they saw the change, they all shrugged their shoulders, commenting absent mindedly: well, it is hard to say, but all we know is that more and more people are going out for more and more drinks.

Now does this leave us with a Helsinki time, which alternates, between getting or being drunk and surviving and surveying the consequences? No, not really. What I am referring to is the time immediately after the rush, which was partly about sobering up, and partly about realizing the limitations of such rapid change, which had knocked on the door faster than we had wished. This change was not only about the economy starting to grow again so that people got proper, well-paid jobs, kids and mortgages. To remain faithfully at the clean and tidy macro level, my claim is that the sobering effect has, again, mostly to do with numbers.

What we did forget is that Helsinki is and will always stay outside the center. The city will remain defined by its location as a relative periphery, which is not, god forbid, straightforwardly exotic, but something else. I mean, currently you find all the same symbols and youth and club culture items and infrastructures in Helsinki as in other European cities. But still, Helsinki has its own flavor, its own character, and its own, yes, smell. It is nearly exotic.

And it is going to stay so, because numbers rule. What this means is that Helsinki is and will remain a city with little more than 0.5 million inhabitants. True, greater Helsinki is growing, with circa 1.5 million people, but the 'true' urban area as such is small, and it is a place with a relatively short history as an active city space. As an urban space concerned with and connecting not only certain marginal groups but also the whole of society, it has not existed longer than twenty years.

Thus, the fertile soil from which to build Helsinki, is not terribly deep. By and large, attitudes are still overwhelmingly anti-city. A current phenomena making waves in the generation born between 1935 and 1945, people now close to pensionable status, is to move back in flocks to their places of origin in the countryside. Consequently, it is not that common to find people in Helsinki who have been living in the city for more than one to two generations.

But do I think this claustrophobic smallness and lack of urban history is a problem? Of course it is not, but it does set limitations, which one must be aware of. Taken in perspective, it is not a problem, because I strongly sense that there is no way of going back. For sure, about 50% of the Finnish population dedicatedly gaze towards the past, towards the illusion of the idyll of an undisturbed, direct contact with nature, while the rest of us continue to try to shape and make an urban environment in which it makes sense to be and to participate.

My belief is based partly on the fact of how friends of mine, me included, view their relationship to Finland and Finnishness. Admittedly, in the 80s, the only way was to get out of the country. Fast. Today, there is no rush to move anywhere. There is no need to deny one's background, or one's identity as a Finn. In fact, and this sounds utterly silly indeed, I believe that most of us thirty-somethings would semi-soberly claim to be proud of being Finnish. The difference is that while before we were able to frequently witness moves on the part of many Finns to pathetically, desperately claim to be 'good' Europeans, today I think most of these sour, unnecessary, uncertainties have evaporated.

In other words, we have a new image with a load of substance. It is the look of love. No longer stuck with the past, or hysterically trying to be hyperactive in the present, the urban Helsinkian is freed of these loadstones. They have now just moved on, got their act together. This moving on, linking back to the personal micro level, is very much in evidence in all the works displayed in this exhibition. Being proud of one's background is not, I hope, nationalistic, as this attitude is used to confront the nation, and to not make us subservient to it. It is a grown-up, constructively critical version of what it means to be a Finn. A version which faces the past, and takes it for a walk, and a laugh. A laugh with, not at.

But now, with the end in sight, excuse me, but I just can't resist. I need to return to the bar atmosphere. It shows so well how so much has changed, but remains the same. Most of the bars of the early 90s are still there (some more successful than others), and exactly the same people are visiting them as before.

Quite recently at one of these bars, Finland was played back to me as a funny, ironical nation. It crystallised both the contact and difference between then and now. In the spring of 1995 the nation experienced a catharsis. A huge drunken crowd witnessed how the national ice hockey team, *The Lions,* won its very first world championship. It was, well, something else. Something deeply important. This spring, Finland was again in the finals, and the same people with the same spirit were in the bars again. This time Finland lost, but this time it was slightly different. The point is that it did not matter.

Where there is Light there is also Shadow
Current Finnish Installation Photography

Caryn Faure Walker

RAINBOW

Between 1997 and 2000, three of the artists under discussion photographed Helsinki's historic theatres and cinemas. Marjaana Kella shot the Auditorium (1997) in the Aleksanterin teatteri; Ola Kolehmainen made Cinema (2000), (illustration pp 46–47), in the 1930s Bio Rex cinema and Jyrki Parantainen constructed a life-size mock cinema as a photographic stage set. The works are all very large format chromogenic colour photographs. The mounting of the pictures (whether on aluminium, or sandwiched in a plexiglass laminate, or made as a series of light boxes) adds an object-like quality to the photographs. The transparent skin covering each image's high colour makes it jewel-like.

The images themselves depict neither people nor events. Instead there are rows of empty seats awaiting an audience. The air bound energy around the seats is what attracts the artists since in this trio of images their cameras magically record the invisible.

Going beyond discussions of technology, Tony Oursler, the American video artist, in 1999 retraced the history of photography. Beginning with Plato's Timaeus, in which shadows are described as projections of truth unavailable to the senses, Oursler's timeline stops at the recent discovery of "live slow motion".[1] Another more familiar example in his history is the rainbow whose colours are created by refraction and internal reflection of light in raindrops. Christians saw this natural phenomenon as a symbol of the seven sacraments. A man-made phenomenon – the images of colour television – come from a not dissimilar rainbow-like spectrum created by photo conductivity.

What is important about Oursler's list of phenomena (whether natural or lens based) is it's ability to evidence other realities.

There are other pertinent examples which Oursler omitted from his chronology. First, there is the preponderance of 19th century spirit photography in which the spectres of famous people were said to have been captured. Second, there are the practices of mediums and spiritualist themselves. In *Alias Grace*, a novel by Margaret Atwood[2], the protagonist, Grace, accused of murder, is subjected to hypnosis and to psychotherapy which had been recently pioneered by Sigmund Freud. The young neurologist who treats Grace also goes to seances held as entertainments in fashionable drawing rooms of the day.[3]

What typifies the 19th century, and continues to typify our own moment, it must be noted again, is the simultaneous belief in the accuracy of science in the form of photography, and the presence of the vaporous and otherworldly. Here, we need only look to the portrait's ability to immortalise the dead, to push beyond time the ephemeral aspects of the self, an ability inherited by photography from older artforms such as portrait painting and wax figures. Our reaction to these arts is to vacillate between seeing the lifelike and the lifeless in them. This is because we mistake the graven image for the real individual and the artists' materials: stone, the skin of fatty oil paint or the silver grains of photography for sentient being.[4]

Beyond commemoration, the portrait's function has been to picture to society at large as archetypes of the anonymous, famous and infamous. As preparation for her two major series: the *Reverse Portraits* (1995–1997), some forty colour images of individuals with their backs to the camera (illustrations pp 42–43) and *Hypnosis* (1997–2000), three-quarter length portraits of people who Marjaana Kella invited to her studio to be hypnotised (illustrations pp 36, 38, 39), Kella studied the history of Finnish commercial studio portraiture. She also went for reference to August Sander's *People of the 20th Century* (c. 1910–1939), a large body of prints intended to catalogue the epoch's social order in Germany.

Kella's interest in both these approaches encouraged her to revise her ideas about the practice of portrait photography. Her portraits would not be of an individual's character. Instead she began to consider the photographic surface as a membrane between inside and out; hypnosis before the camera might penetrate this divide. Kella said: "My task is to illuminate what is not visible – the not visible and the invisible, which are different. Each can be researched by the photographer through light, shadow and colour…."[5] …"More than this I want to make my photographs about emptiness…."[6] "Once I felt something very special. I was thinking about my breathing and somehow I lost myself, like in a yoga exercise, for example staring at a candle. Suddenly I became the candle. If I can be a candle, I can be anything. If you have this void in this way, you empty out the very heavy understanding from your head – then you have this void, then you have everything."[7]

The Japanese photographer, Hiroshi Sugimoto, produced *In Praise of Shadows*, a photographic series made over a four or five hour exposure period

1   Tony Oursler. "I hate the dark. I love the light." *Introjection: mid-career survey 1976–1999.* Williams College Museum of Art, Massachusetts, USA, 1999, pp 102–111

2   Margaret Atwood. *Alias Grace.* Bloomsbury Publishing PLC, London, 1996

3   For an extensive discussion of these issues see: *Identity and Alterity: Figures of the Body 1895/1995.* 46th Venice Biennale, Masilio Editori s.p.a., Venice, 1995

4   See Carol Armstrong. "From Wax to Silver: Sugimoto's Portrait Gallery" in Baskoff/Spector, *Sugimoto: Portraits.* Guggenheim Museum, New York, 2000

5   Marjaana Kella. Unpublished audio tape conversation with the artist. May 2000

6   Ibid.

7   op. cit.

Where there is Light there is also Shadow

which showed the wind's movement around a flame. In an interview,[8] Sugimoto referred this work to Gerhard Richter's earlier paintings of the same subject *Kerze (Candle) I–III* (1982) which Richter remade in 1982–1983 as photo studies for his major work *Atlas, Photographs, Collages and Sketches* (1962–). The shared image of the candle is important in so far as it suggests that Kella, Sugimoto and Richter see light as emblematic of the invisible, the void.

Kella also shares with Sugimoto and Richter her approach to image making. On this point Kella is adamant: "I frame the pictures consciously … using a large format camera with a 210 mm lens, I took some sixteen prints of each subject for the *Hypnosis* images. It was important that the set-up for all the works stayed the same insofar as they all were taken with a short depth of field and uniform lighting … I rarely crop the final images. What interests me in the images is detail, the sitter's gestures, and colour; grey is a colour that is extremely important to me."[9]

At another level it underwrites a common conceptual approach to image making. About this Kella is adamant: "I frame the pictures consciously…. Using a large format camera with a 210 mm lens, I took some sixteen prints of each subject for the *Hypnosis* images (illustrations pp 36, 38, 39). The conventions of a portrait photographer which I use are only necessary as a starting point. Hypnosis splits open these conventions so that the spectator can sense what had previously remained unseen."[10]

In her 2001 Valokuvagalleria Hippolyte installation, Kella made these elements into a pure stillness. She designed two rooms of sparsely hung large colour images of equal size. In the gallery's first room there was a park landscape on one wall and a cloud filled mountain landscape on the wall diagonally opposite (illustrations pp 35, 37). At right angles to the mountain landscape was a mirror. Moving through a doorway into the second room, a continuous row of six new larger than life *Hypnosis* images were hung on adjacent walls. At the back of the room, two men and four women gesticulated towards the camera in a state of hypnosis, their coloured clothing offset by an empty grey back ground.

Each room's display of images at Hippolyte offered the viewer different possibilities of rootedness or disembodiment. The observer might care to stay present in the room's space, to climb into the illusion of the photograph, or to dwell in the mirror's reflection. These alternative possibilities unsettled any pre-suppositions held about photographic realism. The installation also hinted at a wholeness of being which is found in Eastern philosophy, for example in the discussion of colour in the *Tao-te-ching*. Important to Kella's body of work as a whole, it is worth quoting the passage at length:

"Greyness or colorlessness is, as illustrated respectively in a color wheel or prism, the eventual and original reality of colors. It is negative in appearance but decidedly positive in potential. It is not seen as color, but it is colors…. Furthermore, the more greyness a color has, the more it loses its tangible being…."[11]

'Harmonize with the light,
Sympathize with its dustiness.
This is the way of natural
unity.'[12]

FRENCH WINDOWS

"In France, the window is without exception, even in the poorest house, a porte-fenetre, a 'French window' opening to the floor."[13] Entrance and exit, it is also the main aperture for light. Glass gives the window its transparent quality, a sense that inside and out interpenetrate. In 19th century Paris and London, industrial architecture extended the window's transparency by innovative use of iron made into armatures for glass buildings. The Eiffel Tower, Les Halles, the Great Exhibition Hall, other city arcades and department stores, became emblematic of the then unfamiliar rush of crowds, proximity of strangers, the city as a place of irresistible display of goods for consumption.

Interestingly, Ola Kolehmainen's series, *Institut du Monde Arabe* (2001) (illustrations pp 48, 49, 52), uses as its subject windows in a glass building, Institut du Monde Arabe, Paris, designed by Jean Nouvel during the 1980s. Although Kolehmainen was drawn to this landmark, the photographs he made of it do not document the building's style. Nor have the pictures come out of a collaboration between photographer and architect, such as that between Eino Mäkinen and Alvar Aalto in the 1930s (for the Finnish Pavilion at the New

8   Tracey Baskoff. "The Exactness of the World: A Conversation with Hiroshi Sugimoto" in Baskoff/Spector, *Sugimoto: Portraits*. Guggenheim Museum, New York, 2000, pp 34–35

9   Caryn Faure Walker. Unpublished audio tape conversation with the artist. 25 November, 2000

10   Ibid.

11   Amos Ih Tiao Chang. *The Tao of Architecture*. Princeton University Press, Princeton, New Jersey, USA, 1956, p 13

12   Ibid., p14. quotation from Laotzu, *Tao-te-ching*. Shanghai, 1929, vol 307, chapter 56

13   Fritz Stahl. *Paris* (Berlin, 1929 pp 18–19) quoted in: Walter Benjamin. *The Arcades Project; Das Passages Werk (F8a)*. editor Tielemann © 1982, third edition, The Belnap Press, Harvard University Press, Cambridge Massachusetts, USA and London, England

York Worlds Fair)[14] or in the 1990s, the collaboration between the German photographer Thomas Struth and the Swiss architects Herzog and de Meuron. This glass building far from from Helsinki nonetheless mesmerised Kolehmainen; the built environment abroad made him better understand the meaning of architecture at home.

Relevant to Kolehmainen's photographic series, *Institut du Monde Arabe* and to his newest, site-specific installation in the Bio Rex Cinema, *Yellow Staircase* (2001),[15] is the work of the great Finnish architect, Alvar Aalto. Aalto's conception of buildings as a continuous space between nature and habitation mirrored that of the *"pilotos grid* of Le Corbusier, the 'clear' structure of Mies van der Rohe, and the floating planes of De Stijl … [whose] 'free plan' represented freedom from the social, cultural and physical constraints of the old hierarchical order…."[16] From love of Nordic light and Finnish forests, Alvar Aalto inflected this philosophy with regional elements in which windows and rooflights "express[ed] Nordic light as an atmosphere filtered by clouds and foliage."[17]

In *Yellow Staircase,* Kolehmainen pictures the famous stairway from Alvar Aalto's Paimio Sanatorium. Kolehmainen radically scales up this image importing it as a giant photowall into the 1930s Lasipalatsi (Glass Palace) in Helsinki. The staircase motif first appeared in *Portaikko –Trappan* (1999) (illustration p 51), a blue staircase Kolehmainen photographed in Tokyo, which later became part of the larger installation, *Pyramid* (1999), made for Zinc Gallery, Stockholm (illustration p 50). In this installation the large back-lit image of the blue staircase is hung in the final room. Before seeing the image, visitors pass through two introductory rooms where free-standing walls of gold leaf, black plexiglass and blue light radiate (or absorb) light. The use of construction materials as conductors of light is also something that Kolehmainen shares with Aalto.

Whereas the earlier installation *Pyramid* offers silence and stillness, *Yellow Staircase* fuses an idea of movement in an urban environment and indefinable space. The giant 615 cm x 510 cm back-lit digital photograph of Aalto's staircase can be seen directly behind a vast curtain window in the Bio Rex Cinema. Anyone approaching the building sees Kolehmainen's photowall appear to climb through the roof to the sky. On entering the building people regain their sense of gravity as they ascend the stairs to the movie theatre.

The placement of *Yellow Staircase* in Helsinki's Lasipalatsi (Glass Palace) reawakens memories of the surprising effects of the first glass and iron buildings. The most extensive visual topology of these structures has been created by the German photographers, Bernd and Hilla Becher over the last thirty years of the 20th century. To understand how the social world changed because of the appearance of such building technology one must turn to the writings of two German philosophers and architectural historians: Sigfried Giedion particularly his book *Iron Construction* (1907) and Walter Benjamin in *The Arcades Project* (1928 to 1940).

Both men agreed that iron and steel buildings because of their transparency evoked a technical sublimity "which opened to the eye a shadowless extension of space in which subject and object became interwoven."[18] The new reality, Benjamin proposed, was also made available by inventions such as the microscope or camera. Just as dream images acted as rebuses or picture puzzles whose latent content must be revealed, so too "would the close-up in photography reveal … entirely new structural formations of the subject matter…."[19] As these structural formations became available to the mass of people, so too Benjamin thought they would awake from the dreams of consumption of industrial capitalism.

Why this element of Benjamin's social philosophy is pertinent to Kolehmainen's photographic series, *Institut du Monde Arabe*, is that the quality of light and transparency in his photographs of windows imply modernist architecture's openess. Modernism's failure to deliver a brave new world is also implied in the series via a hard cold beauty of surface and blankness. A written exchange between Jean Nouvel, architect of *Institut du Monde Arabe* and Jean Nouvel's mentor, the philosopher Paul Virilio, encapsulates these contradictory stances.

In this exchange Nouvel links his conception of transparency to the speed of modern knowledge, what he has called: "the bi-dimensional registration of visual information: TV, cinema and advertising … [because of which he] found very interesting the qualities of "… glass as a material where you can project images, operate with different degrees of reflection, opacity, transparency."[20] Virilio responds: "Jean Nouvel is not as usually pretended an architect of the

14   Maija Häivä. "Architectural Photography Record or Art," in *Heroism and the Everyday Building, Finland in the 1950s*. Editor-in-Chief Ritta Nikula, Museum of Finnish Architecture, Helsinki 1994, p 255

15   Commissioned for Helsinki Festival, Summer 2001

16   Richard Weston. *Alvar Aalto*. Phaidon Press Limited, London, 1995, p 124

17   op. cit. p 128

18   Detlef Mentins. "Walter Benjamin and the Tectonic Unconscious: Using Architecture as an Optical Instrument", in *The Optic of Walter Benjamin*. Edited by Alex Coles, Volume 5, de-, dis-, ex-, Black Dog Publishing Limited, London, 1999, p 211.

19   Walter Benjamin. "The Work of Art in the Age of Mechanical Reproduction," in *Illuminations*. English translation, 1968, Harcourt, Brace and World Inc. quoted in Detlef Mentins, op. cit. p 207

Where there is Light there is also Shadow

media, but a MEDIATOR between the *real space* of building and the real time of transmission of forms and figures of urban collapse." [21]

MOSKVA BAR

Look for sagging yellow curtains and a piece of paper stuck to the window to find the weirdest bar in Helsinki. Moskva, in Eerikinkatu 11, is a tiny place crammed with Soviet memorabilia that succeeds in having a truly musty East European flavour. This simulacrum of Russian life – which includes stale cheese sandwiches – was founded by the Kaurismäki Brothers, who were not only successful film makers in their own right, but who in 1981 established the film production company, Villealfa. [22]

In the early days of Moskva, Jyrki Parantainen used to drink there with his friends, unsurprising, since the subject of Russia continues to haunt the artist. During the 1970s, Parantainen's father, a socialist, had discussed with his son the pros and cons of the Soviet system. At the time, the official line was to admire the Soviet Union. However, according to Parantainen, "everyone else saw them as a big bear watching us." [23]

In "The Look of Love – The Phenomena of Urbanisation in 1990s Helsinki", Mika Hannula attaches statistics to the attitudes of the Finnish people to the Soviet Union. He says: "Numbers, like diamonds, are man's best friend. In the early 1990s, Finland was, to put it plainly, in a huge political mess…. In relation to the economy, the disappearance of the Communist bloc was even more disastrous…. When in 1991, almost half of Finnish exports were to the Soviet Union, the export market to the USSR collapsed drastically in 1992. What did not drop was the level of unemployment which sky-rocketed from 4% to 5% to more than 20% during 1993–1994." [24]

There are a number of films which Parantainen saw that looked back to Wold War II. *The Unknown Soldier* (Edvin Laine, 1955), *The Boys* (Mikko Niskanen, 1962) and *Winter War* all of which helped the artist understand Finland's paradoxical relationship with the Soviet Union. In addition the artist deeply admired the Russian film maker Andrey Tarkovsky, whose aesthetics of shock suggested that truth came from a violent rupture of the familiar. [25] It is perhaps for this reason that he became convinced by 1989 that his photographic practice would be largely determined by film. [26]

Parantainen also strongly believed that: "in reality the most direct political acton is to influence an individual." [27] Mika Hannula puts it differently: "[It] is a form of Finnishness where the focus is on trying to be as good a Finn as possible … beginning in oneself and one's context even if this by necessity happens via comparison and adaptation from others." [28]

To renew identity is for Parantainen and Hannula to have direct experience, which in turn is the material of art. This philosophy underpins the making of Parantainen's large cycle of works, *Tuli* (Fire) (illustrations pp 65–68).

Between 1993 and 1998 Parantainen and his team of collaborators on the project, Joakim Eskilden, Ola Kolehmainen and Sami Luukkanen, made location shots for *Tuli* (Fire) which was completed in three phases. From 1993 to 1994 the team photographed a deserted mining complex in Outokumpu, central Finland; in 1995 to 1996 they travelled to Tallinn, Paldiski and Haapsalu, Estonia, where they made and photographed the burning of small scale stage sets in former homes of the Russian military. And in 1997 to 1998, the team made more complicated sets, placed them in an abandoned industrial space in central Helsinki and photographed the sets in flames.

Twenty-six images in over thirty-five free standing light boxes, the largest of which measures two and half metres in height and eight and one half metres in length comprise the final work. The huge light boxes are meant to be viewed from each side. At the front of each box is a back-lit image; at the rear, there is an illuminated block of text and image, which provides documentation on the process of making the work. Information on the front and back of the boxes is sometimes contradictory, sometimes consistent. A mode that Parantainen calls "fiction that looks like documentary." [29]

Tuli (Fire) *22.2.98, Helsinki, Finland (No. 29.)*, the penultimate work in the cycle, is directly related to Parantainen's commitment to the cinema. The image

20   Alejandro Zaeva. "Incorporating: interview with Jean Nouvel," in *1987–1998, Jean Nouvel*, third edition, Croquis Editorial, Madrid, 2000, p 31

21   Ibid., Paul Virilio. "To Jean Nouvel," in *1987–1998, Jean Nouvel*, p 337

22   Tytti Solia. "Finland," in *Nordic National Cinemas*. Routledge, London and New York, 1998, p 75

23   Caryn Faure Walker. Unpublished audio tape conversation with the artist. April, 2001

24   Mika Hannula. "The Look of Love: The Phenomenon of Urbanisation in 1990s Helsinki," in *Magnetic North: Current Finnish Installation Photography*. University of Art and Design Helsinki, Helsinki, 2001, p 9

25   For a more extensive discussion of Parantainen's interest in the sublime see: Jyrki Parantainen. *The Artist in flames*. Unpublished Licentiate Thesis. University of Art and Design Helsinki, Department of Photography, Helsinki, 1999, p 27, and Andrei Tarkovsky. *Sculpting in Time*. The Bodley Head, London, 1986

26   Caryn Faure Walker. Unpublished audio tape convensation with the artist. April, 2001

27   Caryn Faure Walker. Unpublished audio tape conversation with the artist. May, 2000

28   Mika Hannula. *Self-Understanding as Process: Understood through the concept of Self-Understanding as a Narrative Form, the Third Dimension of Power, Coming to Terms with the Past, Conceptual Change and Case Studies of Finnishness*. University of Turku, Turku, 1997, p 177

on the front of this light box represents the stage set of a cinema which Parantainen built. On the reverse side are smaller, black-lit photographs of the bare concrete room that houses the set. A movie screen, wall lights, a movie projector beam and tongues of flame partly illuminate the projection theatre. On screen there is a sunlit landscape from *Urga,* (1991) Nikita Mikhalkov's film which describes a chance meeting between a Russian worker laying roads in the tundra and a Mongolian shepherd about to be displaced by this new infrastructure.

Another work in the cycle, *Tuli* (Fire) *Helsinki Finland 23.2.1997,* pays homage to the German painter Anselm Kiefer's *Der Maler's Atelier* (The Artist's Studio) (illustration p 65) Parantainen shot two further colour images in the same location: *Tuli,* (Fire) *Helsinki, Finland, 22.2.1998* (illustration p 68) and *Tuli* (Fire) *Helsinki, Finland, 25.2.1998.* Both show a combined kitchen – study, first intact, then as ashen filth. On the wall is a copy of Yves Klein's *Monogold* series.

The precious material of Klein's work and the kitchen and study in flames suggest that Parantainen, like Kiefer, draws parallels between the roles of artist and alchemist in which a continuum is made between spirit, matter and states of mind. The *Chemical Wedding,* one of many emblems of this process, is symbolised in alchemical drawings by the union of animal, human or celestial forces. Via such union the alchemists foresaw the healing of an ailing physical world and unification of a divided self. Against this utopian aspect of alchemy Parantainen intentionally sets insatiable desire which erupts in flames.

 In the *Mystery of Satisfaction I–VIII* (2001) (illustrations pp 69–73), Parantainen's newest series, he replaces this approach with more immediate image making of his own possessions and of Helsinki restaurants, shops and museum interiors. The finished works, which comprise enlarged details of the original, are single images or abutting diptychs or triptychs. The format in which they are presented is C-type prints mounted on aluminium and laminated. The largest, *The Mystery of Satisfaction No. 2,* 90 cm x 260 cm, is the size of a cinema screen.

This and the earlier series have much in common. The most direct connection can be seen in the erosive quality of flames throughout the *Tuli* (Fire) cycle; and similarly in *The Mystery of Satisfaction No. 4,* time can be seen to have eaten away at a print of Venetian lovers.

Parantainen comments that he invites his viewers to construct an interpretation of his works from a wide range of suggested meanings: "I would underestimate my audience if I were to simplify what I see around me; it is full of complexity. I try to avoid being a propagandist, still I want to participate in the discussion of issues that concern everybody – for example, relief from poverty; how power, violence and gender are used. I think of this approach as the 'politics of multiplicity', a strategy of giving strong opinions about themes I'm handling without closing down meaning. I of course know, at the same time, that the price of this strategy is to risk offering too much complexity – of not being understood at all."

He goes on: "I want both series to have a counterpoint working between visual richness (beauty) and presence (or possible appearance) of horror or violence. To make people curious and to invite them to look at my work I offer them visual richness: colourful surfaces, textures, details and materials.

This is why I find many films, for example David Lynch's, *Lost Highway* (1996), so effective. Its atmosphere is simultaneously frightening and even oppressive, but also astonishingly beautiful. Throughout the film there is darkness and also impenetrable shadows, which are accompanied by a low bass sound that gives the film a dreamlike quality. In contrast, there is incredible lushness of colour – red and yellow fields, the appearance of almost abstract areas. Even though the camera moves inside a small apartment, it flows from monochromatic colour fields to small details." His characters, who speak with extreme economy, are bizarre.[30]

The broken narrative in Parantainen's *The Mystery of Satisfaction* links with the artist's desire for multiple interpretation of his work. The question of what happens next is played out through a number of clues across the images.

For example, the recurring presence of wild, stuffed animals is a tribute to the English film maker Peter Greenaway and his preoccupation with political and erotic power. The suspended animation in which Parantainen pictures the animals is emblematic of a strange 'half-life' of unpleasant pleasures symbolised throughout *The Mystery of Satisfaction* by the colour red. The red of love. The red of blood and violence. Red curtains are a kitsch reference to the Eastern bloc countries with which the artist is so concerned. Intoxicated by the colour we immerse ourselves in its sticky substance with our eyes.

WITTGENSTEIN'S TONGUE

Leena Saraste has written about a dispute amongst Finnish photographers which stretched over more than five decades: should they experiment with the medium, concentrate on composition or record people and events?[31]

29   Caryn Faure Walker. Unpublished audio tape conversation with the artist. May, 2000

30   Jyrki Parantainen. Unpublished email to Caryn Faure Walker. 27 July, 2001

31   Leena Saraste. "Light is ALL, form is all, man is all," in *Valo Mutot Ihminen*. The Finnish Museum of Photography, Helsinki, 2000, pp 75–78

Where there is Light there is also Shadow

By 1978 the availability of fewer jobs for photojournalists in Finland and a new international context for art photography began to tip the balance in favour of the photographer as artist. Ismo Kajander also founded Valokuvagalleria Hyppolite, the first artist run space for photography in Helsinki, whose programme mixed emerging Finnish art and documentary photographers with prominent international artists.

The same year, 1978, the young photographer Jorma Puranen had his first exhibition at the Kluuvi Galleria. A deep interest in visual anthropology convinced Puranen that documentary photography could change things. It was, he said, "more politics than aesthetics".[32]

A decade later in 1988, Puranen visited Finnish Lapland where he was shown black and white photographic portraits of the Sami people. Later, in the Musee de l'Homme, Paris, the artist unearthed an archive of negatives for these prints which he photographed again on large plexiglass panels or polyester sheets. After he journeyed to Northern Norway and Sweden where he re-sited the large format black and white images along centuries old reindeer herding routes which the Sami people had used. Then he further photographed the installations.

Puranen entitled the work *Imaginary Homecoming* (1991–1996). He considered it not only as a symbolic return of the Sami, but also that the final photographs were screens on which viewers could project their fantasies: "The historical portraits … block our path … when we might be tempted simply to admire the beauty of the landscape…. The eyes of the past, so to speak, scrutinise the immense changes that have befallen the northern landscape during the dying century."[33] Today Puranen continues to believe in the availability of history and memory re-invoked by place but mediated by language. This view is clearly present in his *Language is a Foreign Country* (1999–2000), a series that pictures fields of silk flags which carry words articulated in the form of stutter created by the northern climate's turbulent weather.

Puranen was Professor of Photography at the University of Art and Design in Helsinki between 1995 and 1998 where he passed on this belief in the importance of place, identity and language to his students: Elina Brotherus and Andrei Lajunen. By then the economic climate had also changed. The Finnish government was supporting Finnish photography education and photography production. The first exhibitions of Finnish colour photographers of the 1990s were mounted in mainland Europe by the gallerist and educator, Timothy Persons. International demand for contemporary Finnish photography was now emerging. 1998 saw the opening of Kiasma, Helsinki's new Finnish National Gallery of Contemporary Art designed by the architect Steven Holl.

Finally there was a coherent context for Finnish photography, yet the belief that Puranen holds in documentary photography's ability to change things has not been shared by the new generation. Younger photographers like Elina Brotherus and her contemporary Andrei Lajunen (who died in 1999) began to query such ideas.

Just why their questioning arose; and how the zeitgeist which transformed the two artists' beliefs and working methods came to be, is difficult to explain.

Andrei Lajunen had been introduced by Marjaana Kella (his tutor at the University of Art and Design) to Ludwig Wittgenstein's writings on the limit of language to provide a detailed, common understanding of the world. He had re-interpreted this aspect of Wittgenstein's philosophy in favour of a more subjective, anti-theoretical position. In writings on his own work Lajunen said:

"I was and still am interested in colour, above all in an aesthetic sense. I am a colour photographer after all…. Wittgenstein was not interested in that, he wanted to concentrate on the language that we use when talking about colour – the logic of colour codes. This was an interesting point because I realised that colour observations breed in our head. How can we ever be sure we are experiencing them the same way? How can we be sure of observation, senses can always lie."[34] Lajunen's *Tongue*, a part of *The Wittgenstein Portfolio* (c. 1995–1998), engages these tensions. Reproduced as a full colour page in the art magazine *Kuva* (5-6-98), it is a close up of a cow's tongue. The image is a field of pink suction cups that plays on the Finnish word 'kieli' which means tongue and language. Lajunen's photograph not only fuses the concrete with the abstract as does the Finnish word tongue, but also illustrates the impossibility of language to capture the nature of things by naming them.

As the result of her training in analytic chemistry, Elina Brotherus, like Andrei Lajunen tested – and then rejected – the theoretical for the invention of a more informal conceptualism.

Her subject matter is the intimate: close surroundings, her own travel, trusted companions. To show that photography is not magic, in many photographs Brotherus positions herself in front of the camera showing herself holding the camera release chord. She then shoots situations as they arise: "I often work with existing conditions like available light and use objects that happen to be there…. I look for decisive moments, being sensitive and rapid

32 Caryn Faure Walker. Unpublished audio tape conversation with the artist. November, 2000

33 Jorma Puranen. "Foreword" in Jorma Puranen, *Imagined Homecoming*. Pohjoinen, Oulu, Finland, 1999, p 11

34 Andrei Lajunen. Unpublished text to accompany the presentation of the artist's Degree portfolio, c 1998, p 6. Translated from the Finnish by Marianna Collander

when the dense moment is there. It cannot be repeated."[35] Nonetheless, Brotherus is highly conscious as she works: "[the images] are well thought out, I use lots of time to frame the images."[36]

Brotherus' method of making photographs aligns her work with much other photography of the 1980s. Where the two bodies of work part company is that her Anglo-American counterparts have been heavily influenced by film stills, 'real people' advertising and confessional TV programmes. She, instead, has turned for her inspiration to European figurative and landscape painting of the past.

Using European painting in this way, Brotherus choose to consider a variety of issues. In *Landscapes and Escapes* (1997–1999), a series shot primarily in Finland, the relationship between national and individual identity to the landscape was at issue. In *Suites Francaises 1–2* (1999), shot in France, Brotherus used the process of learning French to become more a part of this new country. The pictures wryly show her surroundings pasted with a rash of 'post-it' stickers, her attempt to be in tune with this unfamiliar world of objects and people, not to mention the fresh emotions they sparked.

About her most recent photographs, *The New Painting* (2000) (illustrations pp 26, 27, 28, 30, 31) a series shot in Iceland and Paris, Brotherus writes: "I try with the camera to approach the same problems that painters have been dealing with for centuries: light, colour, composition, figures in space, projection of the three-dimensional into two-dimensional. I find these questions fundamental in all visual arts."[37]

In Spring 2001, the magazine *Paris Photo* (No. 13) published ten images as artist's pages, *Elina Brotherus Photographs 1998–2001* showing figures in interiors and landscapes selected from three previous series: *Das Madchen sprach von Liebe* (1998–99), *Suite Francaises 1* (1999) and *The New Painting* (2000). A similar spread appeared in the summer issue of *Portfolio Magazine* (published in Edinburgh).

When asked in conversation why these works appear together Brotherus replied: "I like all my previous work, any time is as good as any other time." This aside, however casual a comment it may seem, signals a new, more conceptual approach to image making by Brotherus akin to that described by the painter, Gerhard Richter: "I always begin with the intention of obtaining a closed picture with a properly composed motif. Then, with a relatively big effort, I proceed to destroy this intention piece by piece, against my own will almost, until the picture is finished – that is until it has nothing left beside openess."[38]

BRIGHT SHADOW

When referring to himself, the name he used was A. Lajunen. In his mind, there was also the six-legged cat which he invented photographically; it might have insignia for chaos, his notion of how the world was ordered for those creative enough to recognise it.

Then there was the self-portrait. His face was enlarged and shining brightly. His camera was held in position. His face rippled across the surface of a sun-lit oil tanker parked in a car park next to the Helsinki helicopter port, located in a city rust-belt, that he loved to wander through and photograph. One of the last photographs which still remain of A. Lajunen is that of a thirty year old Andrei wearing a 'Suomi' (Finland) T-shirt and looking quizzical, tired. When he had been slightly younger, he had tried out this cowboy image, posing for his self-portrait with a gun.

In March, 1999, I met him very briefly at the Stockholm Artfair where he had just been offered a major exhibition. That summer, about to depart for Japan, he died suddenly of a brain haemorrhage at the age of thirty. After his death I began hunt out the details of his artistic life and attempt to more fully picture who he was. Whomever I spoke with during my search had been deeply affected by him; he was vibrant, even prophetic, as were his photographs.

With the assistance of Andrei Lajunen's parents, the Finnish Museum of Photography and his guardian angel and companion, Nina Pehkonen, there is now an archive of Lajunen's work housed at the FMP which contains several hundred negatives, many proof sheets through which he relentlessly tested colour and image structure. Prior to his study for a Bachelor's Degree in the Photography Department at the University of Art and Design Helsinki, he had studied computer graphics. Impromptu fashions shoots for his fellow students when in Helsinki had stretched Lajunen's skills so that at will he could make beautiful simulations of high fashion and advertising photography which he used to express extremes of elegance and violence.

35   Elina Brotherus. From an unpublished email to Caryn Faure Walker. February, 2000

36   Videotaped interview with Elina Brotherus, commissioned and produced by gb agency, Paris, July 2001

37   Elina Brotherus. Press Statement written for Galleri Stefan Andersson, Umea, Sweden, April 2001

38   Gerhard Ritcher. interview by Benjamin H.D. Buchloh in *Gerhard Richter: Paintings*, ed. Terry Neff, New York, Thames and Hudson, 1998, p 18 as quoted in "Gerhard Richter's Album of Photographs, Collages and Sketches", Armin Zweite in *Photography and Painting in the work of Gerhard Richter, Four Essays on Atlas*, Buchloh/Chernier/Zweite/Rochlitz, Llibres de Recerca, Barcelona, 2nd Edition, 2000, p 98

Where there is Light there is also Shadow

Lajunen was never without his camera; he made images endlessly. However, he hated the idea of selecting a single edit for a series of images. Nina Pehkonen told me a story about Andrei. He had become obsessed by a flower shop full of pink roses. He bought hundreds of the roses and photographed them in a variety of carefully lit studio set-ups as they wilted. For days he walked around everywhere with one hundred small proofs of these images, arranging and re-arranging them.

He came across another of his beloved manifestations of chaos, this time of discarded hospitals beds in a vacant lot in Helsinki. With immense energy he co-opted all his friends and commanded the small army to make a perfect arrangement of organised disarray with the furniture. *Hospital Beds*, (c. 1997–1999) the resulting works, exist in two versions: as a wall hung C-type colour diptych mounted on aluminium, each panel 250 cm x 125 cm; and in portfolio format as a part of Lajunen's *Degree Portfolio* (c. 1999): seventeen panels of different colour images each of whose outside measurement is 51.5 cm x 41 cm.

As Andrei Lajunen wrote extensively about this, before his death, his writing speaks to us from the page:

"I will now explain my thoughts on the work I have done in the first three years. This time has been about searching the boundaries of photography. I hope you will look at the portfolio in peace, a few pictures at a time. One could describe my work so far with the word 'chaos' which is an obsession for logic and order on the reverse side. A certain logic and the lack of theme have, however, turned out to be rather fertile. On the basis of these two aspects, I have for example, made an exhibition consisting of turbulent photographs in Lund, Sweden. Even though my thought in the beginning was themelessness, in the end, one cannot avoid using a certain theme or order because the entire process of selecting the object to the display includes enormous amounts of conscious choice. Naturally, one's own 'figurative handwriting' creates strong unity among the pictures despite the theme.

In my portfolio I have tried to dig into the following questions: categorisation, intuition, narrative, expression, signification, theme-no-theme and coincidence.

Next, I will analyse the content of my portfolio:

A,B,C-area sign photos. Letters and texts are such strong elements that the photos seem to disappear as pictures but if one examines the surface of the picture closely one can find dirt or bullet holes. In the portfolio the ABC-photos also have the role of the signifier. A story is being created. Also the simplest models of logic. On a psychological level the signs indicate agony and fear but also happiness and even awkward simplicity. This is something we all learned even before going to school.

In the police photos I wanted to minimize contact with viewers and therefore cropped the eyes off the photo. In the pictures I study the surface of a fabric or metal or some other form but actually the meaning of the photo is based on strong emotions: power, civil order, safety.

In the photographs taken in a railway car, coincidence steers the situation.

What will probably happen now is that despite the conceptual levels, personal psychological levels win the battle of meanings: subordination and submission, uniform fetishism, voyeurism and other perversions.

Skin-Intimacy. Skin is a universal uniform but here it's apparently the uniform of A. Lajunen.

Next Lajunen himself face to face. Serious expression.

Hospital beds-fears of losing control. Life turns into a mess. Not to the hospital.

Stuffed lion and crushed backside: lost vitality, brutality and sexuality. Replaced with cruelty, violence and the feeling of emptiness-submission.

Lastly a blurry aerial photograph. The truth even begins to fade. Farewell to reality. Hopefully no-one is observing. Why all this analysing with Wittgenstein and others?

A few products of our culture, that have had a great influence on me:

Robert Altman's *Short Cuts*: a film fiction centres on narrative disruption. The film is about the everyday lives and relationships of people who rarely meet or understand each other. In my opinion the film is closer to reality than any other film I've seen without being a document or exact copy of real life like, for example, Warhol's *Empire State Building*. Above all, *Short Cuts* is funny and comical but it incites further speculations on reality and illusion. Is it possible to mime reality? Even though a film or a picture refers to reality is it a part of it as well?

Ludwig Wittgenstein's book: *On Certainty and Remarks on Colour*. As a matter of fact Wittgenstein is notable because he questions and even judges philosophical discussion. We cannot get to the other side of truth with language, why should we even try? If we don't have an idea of the appearance of reality we cannot have the words for it either. Wittgenstein was harsh in saying that everything that can be said can be said clearly.

Ok. We make pictures. When we begin to talk about them and give them meanings it's already speculating – in other words philosophical discussion. What are we doing here? We talk about the meanings of pictures all the time, trying to find explanations."[38]

38   Andrei Lajunen. Unpublished text to accompany the presentation of the artist's Degree portfolio, c 1998, pp 1–6. Translated from the Finnish by Marianna Collander

Elina Brotherus

Marjaana Kella

Ola Kolehmainen

Andrei Lajunen

Jyrki Parantainen

Elina Brotherus

Epiloque
1999
C-type print on aluminium, framed
70 cm x 50 cm

Elina Brotherus

From the New Painting: Horizon 7
2000
C-type print on aluminium, framed
105 cm x 130 cm

From the New Painting: Horizon 8
2000
C-type print on aluminium, framed
105 cm x 130 cm

Elina Brotherus

From the New Painting: Horizon 6
2000
C-type print on aluminium, framed
105 cm x 130 cm

Love Bites II
1999
C-type print on aluminium, framed
70 cm x 56 cm

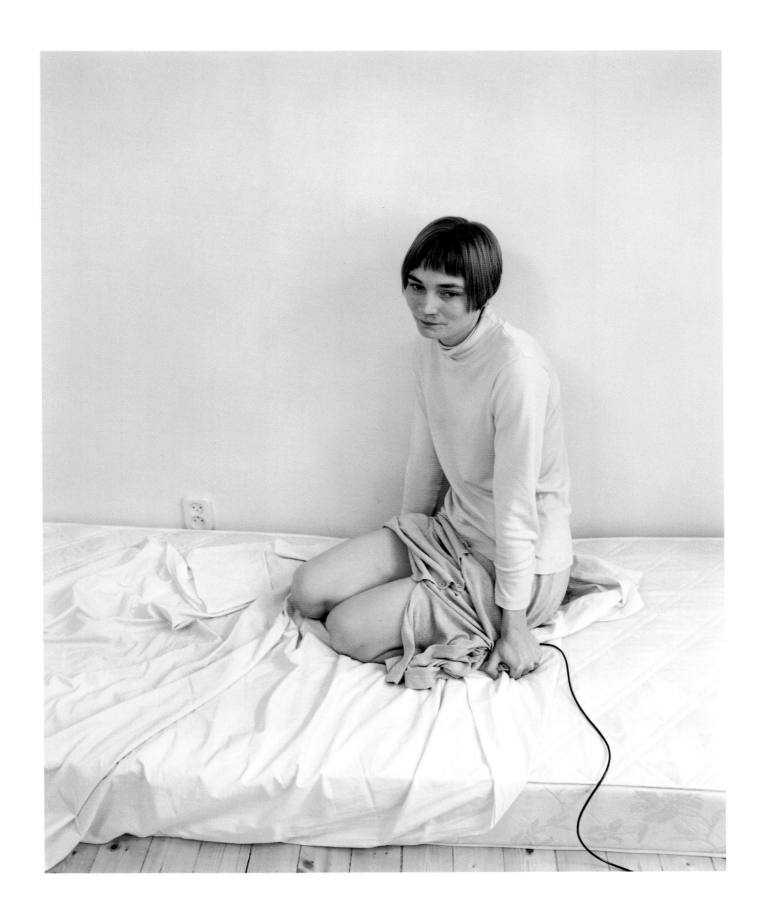

Elina Brotherus

From the New Painting: Homme Derriere Un Rideau
2000
C-type print on aluminium, framed
105 cm x 130 cm

From the New Painting: Femme a Sa Toilette
2001
C-type print on aluminium, framed
80 cm x 60 cm

Elina Brotherus

Le Mirroir
2001
C-type prints on aluminium, framed
40 cm x 32 cm

Marjaana Kella

Mountain, Campo Cecina
2000
C-type print, Diasec
133 cm x 180 cm

Marjaana Kella

Hypnosis: Ritva
2000
C-type print, Diasec
127 cm x 97 cm

Park, Herttoniemi
2000
C-type print, Diasec
133 cm x 180 cm

Marjaana Kella

Hypnosis: Ola
2000
C-type print, Diasec
127 cm x 97 cm

Hypnosis: Tiina
2000
C-type print, Diasec
127 cm x 97 cm

Marjaana Kella

Monte Sumbra
2000
C-Type print, Diasec
170 cm x 125 cm

The Mirror
2000
C-Type print, Diasec
170 cm x 125 cm

Marjaana Kella

Man in a White Shirt
1997
C-type print, Diasec
76 cm x 60 cm

Woman in a Green Cardigan
1997
C-type print, Diasec
76 cm x 60 cm

Man with Eyeglasses
1997
C-type print, Diasec
76 cm x 60 cm

Man in a Red Sweatshirt
1997
C-type print, Diasec
76 cm x 60 cm

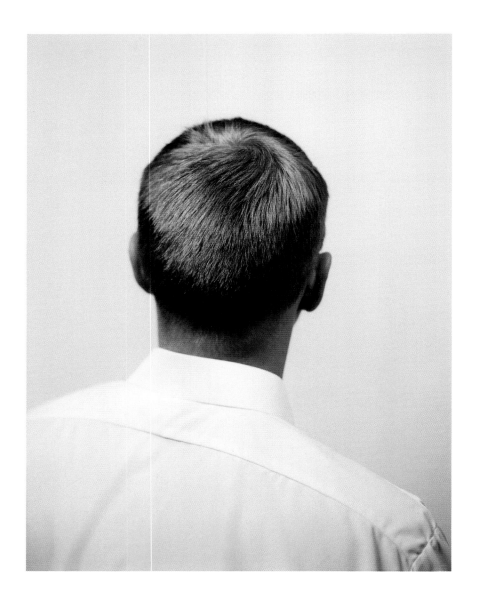
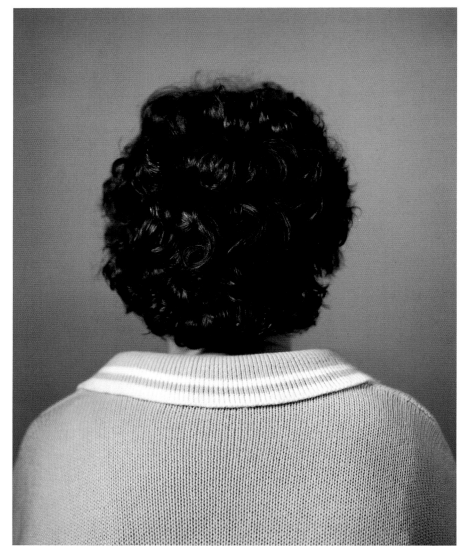

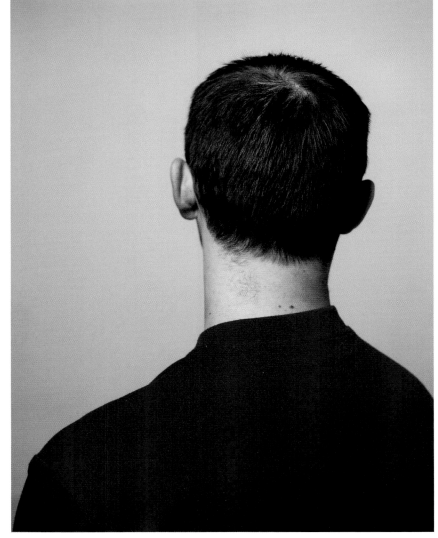

Ola Kolehmainen

The Music is About to Begin
2000
C-type print, Diasec
130 cm x 184 cm

Ola Kolehmainen

Cinema (diptych)
2000
C-type print, Diasec
175 cm x 283 cm

Ola Kolehmainen

Institut du Monde Arabe No. 12
2001
C-type print, Diasec
170 cm x 215 cm

Institut du Monde Arabe No. 14
2001
C-type print, Diasec
170 cm x 216 cm

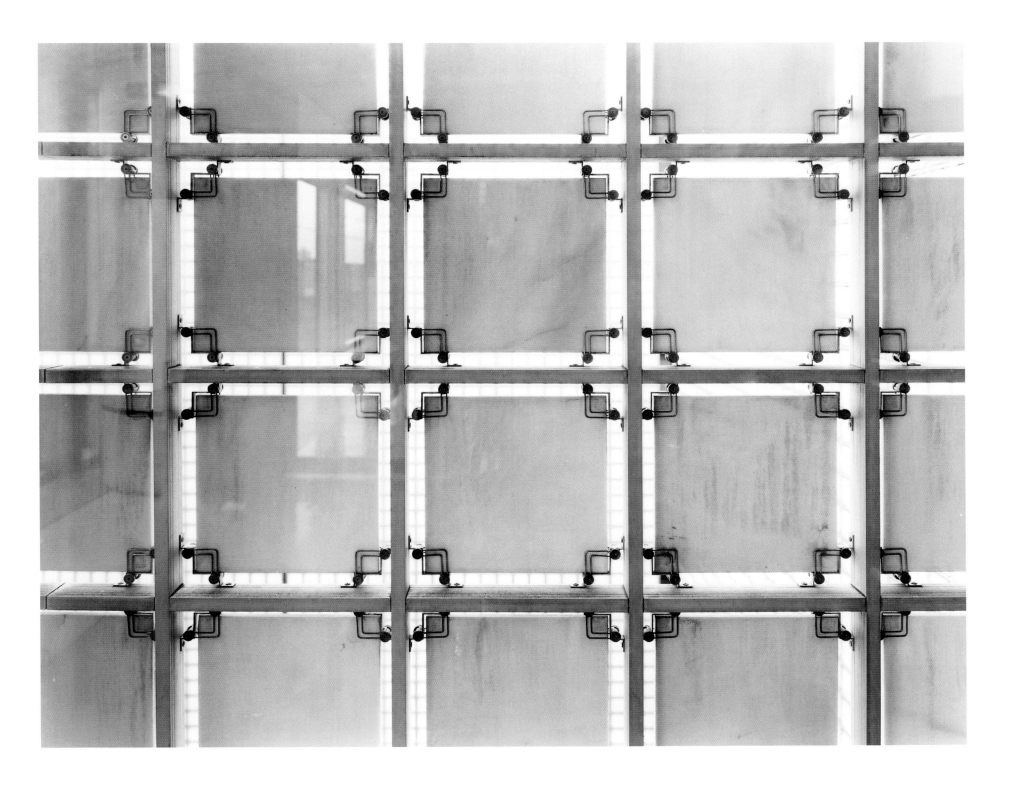

Ola Kolehmainen

Pyramidi: Portaikko–Trappan (Staircase)
1998–1999
Zinc Gallery

Pyramidi: Portaikko–Trappan (Staircase)
1998–1999
Duratrans print, Acrylic light case
170 cm x 160 cm

Ola Kolehmainen

Institut du Monde Arabe No. 11
2001
C-type print, Diasec
170 cm x 222 cm

Air
2001
C-type print, Diasec
140 cm x 209 cm

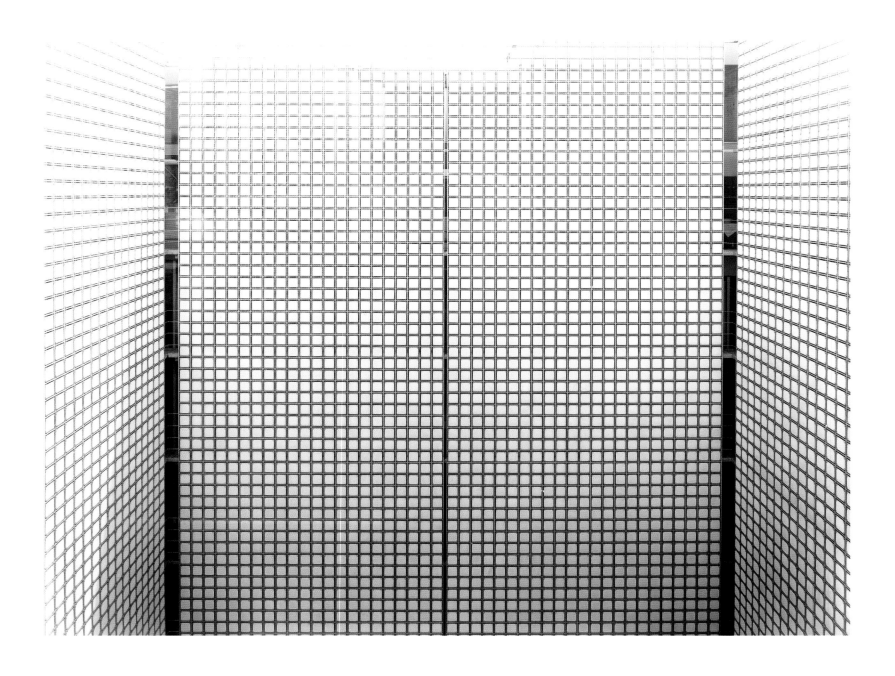

Andrei Lajunen

Untitled (Police Station)
c. 1997–1998
C-type print on aluminium
250 cm x 125 cm
Portfolio print image: 51.5 cm x 41 cm

Andrei Lajunen

Policeman
c. 1997–1998
C-type print on aluminium
47 cm x 37 cm
Portfolio print image: 20 cm x 16 cm

Stage I
c. 1997–1998
C-type print on aluminium
60 cm x 62 cm
Portfolio print image: 33 cm x 33 cm

Andrei Lajunen

Stage II–VI
c. 1997–1998
C-type prints on aluminium
60 cm x 62 cm
Portfolio print images: 13 cm x 13,5 cm

Andrei Lajunen

Policeman
c. 1997–1998
C-type print on aluminium
47 cm x 37 cm
Portfolio print image: 20 cm x 16 cm

Wall
c. 1997–1998
C-type prints on aluminium
47 cm x 37 cm

6

Andrei Lajunen

Untitled (Lion)
c. 1997–1998
C-type print on aluminium
62 cm x 60 cm

Untitled (skin)
c. 1997–1998
C-type print on aluminium
47 cm x 37 cm
Portfolio print image: 34 cm x 33 cm

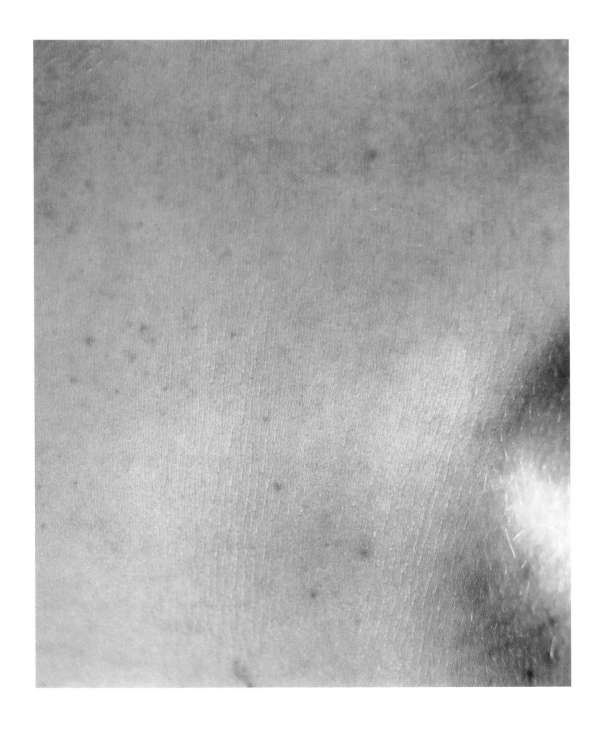

Jyrki Parantainen

Fire, 23.2.1997, Helsinki, Finland
Duratrans print and free standing lightbox
130 cm x 100 cm

Jyrki Parantainen

Fire, 24.5.1998, Helsinki, Finland
Duratrans print and free standing lightbox
175 cm x 260 cm

Jyrki Parantainen

Fire, 22.2.1998, Helsinki, Finland
Duratrans print and free standing lightbox
130 cm x 175 cm

The Mystery of Satisfaction No. 4
2001
C-type print on aluminium
98 cm x 130 cm

Jyrki Parantainen

The Mystery of Satisfaction No. 2
2001
C-type prints on aluminium
80 cm x 274 cm

Jyrki Parantainen

The Mystery of Satisfaction No. 1
2001
C-type print on aluminium
95 cm x 228 cm

ELINA BROTHERUS

Born in 1972, Helsinki, Finland.
Lives and works in Helsinki and Paris.

EDUCATION

2000 Master of Arts (Photography) University of Art and
Design Helsinki

1998 Bachelor of Arts (Photography) University of Art
and Design Helsinki

1997 Master of Science (Analytical Chemistry) University
of Helsinki

SOLO EXHIBITIONS

2002 Hämeenlinna Art Museum, Finland

Encontros da imagem, Braga, Portugal

Västerås Art Museum, Sweden

Orchard Gallery, Derry, Ireland

INOVA (Institute of Visual Arts), Milwaukee,
Wisconsin (catalogue)

Lund Art Hall, Sweden (catalogue)

2001 *Suites Françaises 2*. &: gb agency, Paris (catalogue)

The New Painting. Galleri Stefan Andersson, Umeå,
Sweden

2000 Encontros de Fotografia, Coimbra, Portugal

Suites Françaises 1. Galerie Anhava, Helsinki
(catalogue)

Galleri i8, Reykjavik (catalogue)

Northern Photography Centre, Rantagalleria, Oulu,
Finland

The Finnish Museum of Photography, Helsinki

1998 *Dance Portraits*. Galerie Anhava, Helsinki

Galleri Stefan Andersson, Umeå, Sweden (catalogue)

With Andrei Lajunen, Galerie Anhava, Helsinki

SELECTED GROUP EXHIBITIONS

2001 *ARS 01*. Kiasma, Museum of Contemporary Art,
Helsinki (catalogue)

Théâtres du Fantastique, Printemps de Septembre,
Toulouse, France (catalogue)

*Magnetic North: Current Installation Photography in
Finland*. The New Art Gallery Walsall, England

*Confidences: Parce que c'était moi, Parce que c'était
lui*. Casino Forum d'Art Contemporain, Luxembourg
(catalogue)

Surface and Whirlpools. Borås Art Museum, Borås,
Sweden (catalogue)

Fotofinlandia 2000 Award. Cable Factory, Helsinki

2000 Jahresgaben. Frankfurter Kunstverein, Frankfurt am
Main, Germany (catalogue)

One of those days. Mannheimer Kunstverein,
Mannheim, Germany (catalogue)

*Quinze en Europe, La jeune photographie
européenne*. Nice (catalogue)

Waterfront, Kulturbro 2000. Kulturhuset
Toldkammeret, Helsingør, Denmark, and
Helsingborgs Museum, Sweden (catalogue)

*Narcisse blessé, Autoportraits contemporains 1970–
2000*. Passage de Retz, Paris (catalogue)

*Norden / North, Zeitgenössische Kunst aus
Nordeuropa*. Kunsthalle Wien (catalogue)

Think 2000. 130th Anniversary exhibition of the
University of Art and Design Helsinki. The Finnish
National Gallery Ateneum, Helsinki (catalogue)

Sandroni Rey Gallery, Los Angeles, USA

Galerie Lindig in Paludetto, Nürnberg, Germany

1999 *Tila – Espaces*. Maison Européenne de la
Photographie, Paris

Spaces. The Finnish Museum of Photography,
Helsinki

The Passion and the Wave. 6th International
Istanbul Biennial of Contemporary Art. Turkey
(catalogue)

Identité Fictive, Photographie finlandaise. Espace
photographique Contretype, Brussels 1999 (catalogue)

*Finnish Line: Starting Point, jeunes artistes
finlandais*. Musée d'art moderne et contemporain,
Strasbourg

1998 Galleri Andréhn-Schiptjenko, Stockholm, Sweden

BOOKS

Caryn Faure Walker. *Magnetic North: Current
Installation Photography in Finland*. The Finnish
Museum of Photography and University of Art and
Design Helsinki, Helsinki, 2001

SELECTED ARTICLES AND PUBLICATIONS

Laurie Attias. *Frieze*, Sepember, 2001. London, 2001

Brigitte Kölle. *Portfolio*, No. 33, 2001. Edinburgh,
2001

Søren Haldt. "Elina Brotherus: Behind My Eyes."
Katalog, Vol. 13, No. 2, 2001. Museet for Fotokunst,
Odense, 2001

Françoise-Aline Blain. "Elina Brotherus: Le Français
en dix-huit leçons." *Aden / Le Monde,* 26.4.2001

Michel Guerrin. *Le Monde*, 6.–7.5.2001

Previews: Elina Brotherus, Suites Françaises 2.
Contemporary Visual Arts (CVA), issue 34/2001.
London, 2001

Biographies

Elina Brotherus. "Artiste invitée / Artist Insert." *Paris Photo* No. 13, April–May 2001. Paris, 2001

Michel Guerrin. "Intimité/identité sous l'œil d'Elina Brotherus, 27 ans." *Le Monde*, 22.–23.8.1999

Tuomo-Juhani Vuorenmaa and Jukka Kukkonen, ed. *Valoa: Otteita suomalaisen valokuvan historiaan.* The Finnish Museum of Photography, Helsinki, 1999.

Elina Brotherus. "The Wedding Portraits"; Photographs from the Series "Das Mädchen sprach von Liebe." *Kuva,* No. 3, 1998, Helsinki 1998

WORKS IN COLLECTIONS

Amos Andersson Art Museum, Helsinki

Gothenburg Art Museum, Sweden

Malmö Art Museum, Sweden

Moderna Museet, Stockholm

Musée d'Art Moderne et Contemporain, Strasbourg, France

Musée Nicéphore Niépce, Chalon-sur-Saône, France

Kiasma, Museum of Contemporary Art, Helsinki

Museum of Contemporary Art, Tampere, Finland

Oulu Art Museum, Finland

The Finnish Museum of Photography, Helsinki

Västerås Art Museum, Sweden

Centre National d'Arts Plastiques (CNAP), France

Finnish State Art Collection

Swedish State Art Council

County Councils of Gävleborg, Halland, Jönköping, Uppsala and Västerbotten, Sweden

City of Nice, France

Umeå Municipality, Sweden

Saastamoinen Foundation, Finland

Private Collections in Belgium, Finland, France, Germany, Sweden, Switzerland and the United States of America

MARJAANA KELLA

Born in 1961, Orimattila, Finland.
Lives and works in Helsinki.

EDUCATION

1993   Master of Arts (Photography), University of Art and Design Helsinki

1985–1986 Free Art School, Helsinki

ACADEMIC EXPERIENCE

1993–99 Visiting lecturer at Department of Photography, University of Art and Design Helsinki; The Academy of Fine Arts, Helsinki; Department of Photography, Turku Polytechnic Arts & Media; Department of Photography, Lahti Polytechnic, Institute of Design

SOLO EXHIBITIONS

2003   The Finnish Museum of Photography, Helsinki
2002   Van Zoetendaal Gallery, Amsterdam

The Dutch Photoinstitute, Rotterdam, The Netherlands

Zinc Gallery, Stockholm

Galleria Kari Kenetti, Helsinki

2001   Valokuvagalleria Hippolyte, Helsinki

Galleri Magnus Åklundh, Malmö, Sweden

1999   Hasselblad Center, Gothenburg, Sweden. With Anna Gaskell and Joachim Schmid (catalogue)

1998   Valokuvagalleria Hippolyte, Helsinki

1993   Galleria Finnfoto, Helsinki

SELECTED GROUP EXHIBITIONS

2001   *Magnetic North: Current Installation Photography in Finland.* The New Art Gallery Walsall

Scratches on Smooth Surface. Hasselblad Center, Gothenburg, Sweden

Finnish Photography. Galleri Christian Dam, Oslo

Widening Circle. Kiasma, Museum of Contemporary Art, Helsinki

1999   *Valoa & Varjosta.* The Finnish Museum of Photography, Helsinki (catalogue)

Nordiskt foto. Skövde Konsthall, Sweden

Tila – Espaces. Maison Européenne de la Photographie, Paris

1998   *Blue You.* Into-galleria, Helsinki

Me, Myself and I. Bensow House, Helsinki (catalogue)

1995   *The Play of Living Forms.* Galleria Otso, Espoo, Finland

1993   *Antologia della Fotografia Finlandese una Luce dal Nord.* Rome

Work in Progress. Into-galleria, Helsinki

1992   *Decennium.* Bucharest, Scotland, Istanbul, Ankara, Barcelona, Madrid (catalogue)

1991   *Mesenaatti.* Oulainen, Finland (catalogue)

1989   Nuorten valokuvaajien näyttely (Exhibition of Young Photographers). Helsinki

BOOKS

Pia Sivenius. *Marjaana Kella.* Van Zoetendaal Publications, Amsterdam, 2002

Caryn Faure Walker. *Magnetic North: Current Installation Photography in Finland.* The Finnish Museum of Photography and University of Art and Design Helsinki, Helsinki, 2001

SELECTED PUBLICATIONS AND ARTICLES

Pirkko Siitari. "The Golden Age of Finnish Photography." *Arttu* No. 2, 2001, Helsinki

Alistair Robinson, "Fact, Fiction and Photography." *www.londonart.co.uk magazine,* 2000

Erik van der Heeg. *Face.* Zinc Gallery, Stockholm, 2000

Tuomo-Juhani Vuorenmaa and Jukka Kukkonen, ed. *Valoa: Otteita suomalaisen valokuvan historiaan.* The Finnish Museum of Photography, Helsinki, 1999.

Tuomo-Juhani Vuorenmaa and Jukka Kukkonen, ed. *Varjosta: Tutkielmia suomalaisen valokuvan historiasta.* The Finnish Museum of Photography, Helsinki, 1999.

Tuomo-Juhani Vuorenmaa, ed. *Finnish Photography 1998–1999.* Musta Taide, Helsinki, 1999

Caryn Faure Walker. "Focus on Finland." *Creative Camera,* No. 355, December–January, 1999. London

Marjaana Kella and Marja Söderlund. *Nuori Taide.* Hanki ja jää, Tampere, 1992

Timo Kelaranta. "Marjaana Kella." *Valokuvalehti,* No. 5, 1990. Helsinki

WORKS IN COLLECTIONS

Swedish State Art Council

Hasselblad Center, Gothenburg, Sweden

Helsinki City Art Museum

Malmö Art Museum, Sweden

Kiasma, Museum of Contemporary Art, Helsinki

The Finnish Museum of Photography, Helsinki

County Council of Skåne, Sweden

Private collections in Finland

OLA KOLEHMAINEN

Born in 1964, Helsinki, Finland.
Lives and works in Helsinki.

EDUCATION

1999 Master of Arts (Photography), University of Art and Design Helsinki

1988–92 Department of Journalism, University of Helsinki

SOLO EXHIBITIONS

2002 Galleria Kari Kenetti, Helsinki

2001 *The Yellow Staircase*, site specific public work commissioned by Helsinki Festival

2000 *Golden Hall*. i8 Galleri, Reykjavik

Permanent site specific installation for a restaurant, Helsinki

1999 *Pyramid*, gallery installation. Zinc Gallery, Stockholm

1998 *Portaikko – Trappan*, gallery installation. Galleria Kari Kenetti, Helsinki

1997 *Temple*, gallery installation. Kluuvin Galleria, Helsinki (catalogue)

1996 *Exitus*. Rantagalleria, Oulu, Finland

1995 *Exitus*. Galleria Laterna Magica, Helsinki

Gallery installation, Galleria Finnfoto, Helsinki

1994 *Qinterro*. Galleria Laterna Magica, Helsinki

Torn, portraits. Theatre Pikku Lillan, Helsinki

1992 *Jazz*. Stoa, East Helsinki Cultural Center

SELECTED GROUP EXHIBITIONS

2001 *Magnetic North: Current Installation Photography in Finland*. The New Art Gallery Walsall

Finnish Photography. Galleri Christian Dam, Copenhagen

Finnish Photography, Galleri Christian Dam, Oslo

2000 *100 Show; 90 Designers – 10 Artists*, Helsinki

1999 *Tila – Espaces*. Maison Européenne de la Photographie, Paris

Spaces. The Finnish Museum of Photography, Helsinki

1998 *Blue You*. Into-Galleria, Helsinki

Me, Myself and I. Bensow House, Helsinki (catalogue)

1996 *Fotofinlandia 1996 Award Exhibition*. Helsinki (catalogue)

European Photography Award Exhibition. Bad Homburg, Germany (catalogue)

1995 *Painajainen*. Tampere, Kuopio, Iisalmi and Oulu, Finland

1994 *Planket*. Stockholm (catalogue)

ARTIST BOOKS

Ola Kolehmainen. *Qinterro*. Gravure portfolio. Opus 26, Helsinki, 1994

BOOKS

Caryn Faure Walker. *Magnetic North: Current Installation Photography in Finland*. The Finnish Museum of Photography and University of Art and Design Helsinki, Helsinki, 2001

SELECTED ARTICLES AND PUBLICATIONS

Ola Kolehmainen. Artist's Insert: "Everyday Life and the Touch of the Unknown." *Zoo, Contemporary Culture Catalogue*. London, 1999

Kati Lintonen. *Frames: Viewing Finnish Contemporary Photography*. Frame, Helsinki, 1998

Caryn Faure Walker. "Focus on Finland." *Creative Camera*, No. 355, December–January, 1999. London

Maarit Seeling. "Tenppeli Kluuvissa." *Arkkitehtuuri*, No. 5–6, 1997. Helsinki, 1998

Tuomo-Juhani Vuorenmaa, ed. *Finnish Photography 1996–1997*. Musta Taide, Helsinki, 1997

Kati Lintonen. *Valokuva*, No. 2, 1996. Helsinki

Kati Lintonen. *Valokuva*, No. 4, 1995. Helsinki

Taneli Eskola and Kari Holopainen. *Gravyyrioppi: Syväpainotyötä valokuvaajille ja taidegraafikoille*. Musta Taide, Helsinki, 1995

M. Häyrynen, ed. *Book of Parks in Helsinki*. The Helsinki City Society, Helsinki, 1994

Album covers for Sonet Finland, BMG Finland, Siel on Velvet Record Publishing and Zen Garden Records. 1991–95

WORKS IN COLLECTIONS

Finnish Broadcasting Company

The Finnish Museum of Photography, Helsinki

Helsinki City Art Museum

The Kouri Collections

Lars Swanljung Collections

Swedish State Art Council

Zinc Gallery, Stockholm

Private Collections in Finland, France, Norway and Portugal

ANDREI LAJUNEN

Born in 1969, Joroinen, Finland.
Died in 1999, Helsinki, Finland

EDUCATION

1998 Bachelor of Arts (Photography), University of Art and Design Helsinki

SOLO EXHIBITIONS

1998 With Elina Brotherus. Galerie Anhava, Helsinki

Galleri Magnus Åklundh, Lund, Sweden

SELECTED GROUP EXHIBITIONS

2001 *Magnetic North: Current Installation Photography in Finland*. The New Art Gallery Walsall

2000 Galleri Magnus Åklundh, Malmö, Sweden

1999 *Konst på Hedbergs*. Vinslöv, Sweden

Galleri Magnus Åklundh, Stockholm Art Fair

1997 *Värinä*. Galleria Workshop, Helsinki

Kökar. Galleria Atski, Helsinki

1996 *Aita-Planket*. The Railway Station of Helsinki

1995 *Valoeliöitä*. Museum of Contemporary Art, Tampere, Finland

BOOKS

Caryn Faure Walker. *Magnetic North: Current Installation Photography in Finland*. The Finnish Museum of Photography and University of Art and Design Helsinki, Helsinki, 2001

WORKS IN COLLECTIONS

The Finnish Museum of Photography

City of Lund

Kouri Collection

Private Collections in Finland and Sweden

Biographies

JYRKI PARANTAINEN

Born in 1962 in Tampere, Finland.
Lives and works in Helsinki

EDUCATION

2000   Doctoral Studies (Photography), University of Art and Design Helsinki

1999   Licentiate of Arts (Photography), University of Art and Design Helsinki

1992   Master of Arts (Photography), University of Art and Design Helsinki

ACADEMIC EXPERIENCE

1992–   Lectureship at University of Art and Design Helsinki

SOLO EXHIBITIONS

2000   *Fire*. i8 Galleri, Reykjavik (catalogue)

Fire. The Nordic House, Reykjavik (catalogue)

Fire. Foto & Co, Turin, Italy

Fire. Fotografiska Center, Copenhagen (catalogue)

1999   *Fire*. Contemporary Art Museum, Tampere, Finland

1998   *Fire*. Zinc Gallery in Luma, Stockholm

Fire. The Finnish National Gallery Ateneum, Helsinki (catalogue)

1997   *Earth*. Le Parvis, Tarbes, France (catalogue)

The Sparkling Circle of the Heavenly Host. Installation in public place. Helsinki

1995   *Paldiski*. fc-Galleri, Malmö, Sweden

C2H5 o No, Valokuvagalleria Hippolyte, Helsinki

1993   *Earth*. Galleria Luukku, Joensuu, Finland

1992   *Earth*. Tapetenfabrik, Bonn, Germany, Center of Culture, Turku, Finland, Gallery Elvis, Pori, Finland

1991   *Earth*. Gallery Laterna Magica, Helsinki

SELECTED GROUP EXHIBITIONS

2001   *Magnetic North: Current Installation Photography in Finland*, The New Art Gallery Walsall, England

Chaos and Communication. Curator for the exhibition. National Gallery, Sarajevo, Bosnia Hertzegovina (catalogue)

Aurora. Art Gallery of Sudbury, Canada (catalogue)

Single Room. Trevi Flash Art Museum, Italy (catalogue)

Portfolio. The Finnish Museum of Photography, Helsinki

Finnish Photography. Gallery Christian Dam, Copenhagen

Finnish Photography. Gallery Christian Dam, Oslo

Une Histoire Finlandaise. Galerie Photo, Montpelier, France

2000   *Works from Kiasma Collection*. Tensta Konsthall, Sweden

Aratta. Kopavogur Art Museum, Reykjavik

Big Torino 2000 Biennale. Turin, Italy (catalogue)

International Photographic Exhibition. Alessandria, Italy

1999   *Tila – Espaces*. Maison Européenne de la Photographie, Paris

Auf der Suche nach der Verlorenen Zeit. Haus am Waldsee, Berlin (catalogue)

Spaces. The Finnish Museum of Photography, Helsinki

Focus in Fire. Galerie Nei Liicht, Luxemburg

Biennale de Giovani Artisti dell'Europa del Mediterraneo. Rome (catalogue)

Valoa & Varjosta. The Finnish Museum of Photography, Helsinki (catalogue)

1998   *Me, Myself and I*. Bensow House, Helsinki (catalogue)

Underexposed. Stockholm (catalogue)

1997   *Romeo Martinez International Award*. San Marino (catalogue)

The Drum and the Camera. Gallen Kallela Museum, Espoo, Finland (catalogue)

Paysages et Matières. NCE, Paris

Photographies pour une Itinerance. NCE, Paris

Momentum. The Finnish Museum of Photography, Helsinki

Enter. Taidehalli, Helsinki

Reflections in Circle. Aberdeen, Scotland

1995   *The Play of Living Forms*. Galleria Otso, Espoo, Finland

Vents du Nord. Bibliothèque H. Vincenot, Talant, France

Mai de la Photo. l'Ancien College des Jesuites, Reims, France (catalogue)

3 Photographers from Finland. The Photography Museum, Tallinn, Estonia

Finnish Images in Print. Eirmos Art Gallery, Thessaloniki, Greece

Northern Realities. Macedonian Museum for Contemporary Art, Thessaloniki, (catalogue)

Ateneumin Taidemuseo (The Finnish National Gallery Ateneum), Helsinki

1992   *Finlandida-92*. Konstakademien, Stockholm (catalogue)

Decennium. Bucharest, Scotland, Istanbul, Ankara, Barcelona, Madrid (catalogue)

Painettu Valokuva (The Printed Photograph). Gallery Zebra, Karjaa, Finland

56 Nord. Loppehallen, Århus, Denmark

1990   *Fotofinlandia 1989 Award Exhibition*. Valokuvagalleria Hippolyte, Helsinki

1988   *Nuori Suomi* (Young Finland). Retretti, Punkaharju, Finland

ARTIST BOOKS

Jyrki Parantainen, R. Kovalainen and K. Holopainen. *Gaia*. Silver print portfolio. University of Art and Design Helsinki, Helsinki, 1993

Jyrki Parantainen. *Maa* (Earth). Offset lithography portfolio. Opus 18, Helsinki, 1991

Jordi Guaridor (alias Jyrki Parantainen). *Uns Tretze Petits Catalans*. Offset lithography portfolio. Helsinki, 1987

BOOKS

Caryn Faure Walker. *Magnetic North: Current Installation Photography in Finland*. The Finnish Museum of Photography and University of Art and Design Helsinki, Helsinki, 2001

Mari Krappala. *Burning (of) Ethics Of The Passion: Contemporary art as a process*. Doctoral Thesis. University of Art and Design Helsinki, Helsinki, 1999

Jyrki Parantainen. *The Artist in Flames: The Flame, The Sublime and My Art*. Literary Part of Art-Emphasised Licenciate Thesis. University of Art and Design Helsinki, Helsinki, 1999

SELECTED ARTICLES AND PUBLICATIONS

Ute Noll, "Spiel mit dem Feuer." *Frankfurter Rundschau*, May 20th, 2000. Franfurt

Pia Strandman, ed. *Ateneum maskerad: Taideteollisuuden muotoja ja murroksia. Taideteollinen korkeakoulu 130 vuotta*. University of Art and Design Helsinki, Helsinki, 1999

Tuomo-Juhani Vuorenmaa, ed. *The Art of Photography: Photography in Finland 1998–1999*. Musta Taide, 1999. Helsinki

Caryn Faure Walker. "Focus on Finland." *Creative Camera*, No. 355, December–January, 1999, London

Joyce Mason. "Jyrki Parantainen: FIRE." *C-Magazine*, September–November, 1998

Paul Steen. "Pyromani." *Dagens Nyheter*, September 18, 1998, Stockholm

Mari Krappala. "Everyday Life and the Touch of the Unknown" *Frames: Viewing Finnish Contemporary Photography*. Frame, Helsinki, 1998

Leena Saraste. *Photography – Between Tradition and Reality*, Musta Taide/University of Art and Design Helsinki, Helsinki, 1996

Jukka Kukkonen and Tuomo-Juhani Vuorenmaa, ed. *Valokuvan Taide: Suomalainen valokuva 1842–1992*. SKS, Helsinki, 1992

WORKS IN COLLECTIONS

Amos Andersson Art Museum, Helsinki

Bibliothèque Nationale de France, Paris

Grenoble Artheteque, Grenoble, France

Lahti City Art Museum, Lahti, Finland

Maison Européenne de la Photographie, Paris

Mois de la Photo, Montreal

Kiasma, Museum of Contemporary Art, Helsinki

The Finnish Museum of Photography, Helsinki

The Museum of Fine Arts, Houston

The Finnish State Art Collection

Espoo City Art Collection, Espoo, Finland

Kodak Company, Finland

Bibliothèque H. Vincenot, Talant, France

Dorint Hotel, Brussels

Henna and Pertti Niemistö Foundation, Finland

Saastamoinen Collection, Kuopio, Finland

Pétur Arason Art Collection, Reykjavik

Private Collections: Denmark, Finland, France, Germany, Greece, Sweden, Italy, Norway, USA

Magnetic North: Current Installation Photography in Finland
The New Art Gallery Walsall, 28 September to 16 November, 2001

1. ELINA BROTHERUS
    From the New Painting: Horizon 6
    2000
    C-type print on aluminium, framed
    105 cm x 130 cm

2. ELINA BROTHERUS
    From the New Painting: Horizon 7
    2000
    C-type print on aluminium, framed
    105 cm x 130 cm

3. ELINA BROTHERUS
    From the New Painting: Horizon 8
    2000
    C-type print on aluminium, framed
    105 cm x 130 cm

4. ELINA BROTHERUS
    The Fundamental Loneliness
    1999
    C-type print on aluminium, framed
    70 cm x 50 cm

5. ELINA BROTHERUS
    Epilogue
    1999
    C-type print on aluminium, framed
    70 cm x 50 cm

6. ELINA BROTHERUS
    This is the first day of the rest of your life.
    1998
    C-type print on aluminium, framed
    70 cm x 88 cm

7. ELINA BROTHERUS
    I hate sex.
    1998
    C-type print on aluminium, framed
    80 cm x 110 cm

8. ELINA BROTHERUS
    Landscapes and Escapes I
    1997
    C-type print on aluminium, framed
    105 cm x 130 cm

9. ELINA BROTHERUS
    From the New Painting: Femme à Sa Toilette
    2001
    C-type print on aluminium, framed
    80 cm x 66 cm

10. ELINA BROTHERUS
    From the New Painting: Homme Derrière Un Rideau
    2000
    C-type print on aluminium, framed
    105 cm x 130 cm

11. ELINA BROTHERUS
    Love Bites I
    1998
    C-type print on aluminium, framed
    70 cm x 56 cm

12. ELINA BROTHERUS
    Love Bites II
    C-type print on aluminium, framed
    1999
    70 cm x 56 cm

13. ELINA BROTHERUS
    Love Bites III
    1999
    C-type print on aluminium, framed
    70 cm x 56 cm

14./15. ELINA BROTHERUS
    From the New Painting: Deux Personage dans un Paysage
    2000
    C-type print on aluminium, framed
    70 cm x 89 cm

16.–20. ELINA BROTHERUS
    Le Mirroir
    2001
    C-type print on aluminium, framed
    40 cm x 32 cm

21. ELINA BROTHERUS
    Les Baigneurs
    C-type print on aluminium, framed
    2000
    70 cm x 89 cm

22. MARJAANA KELLA
    Mountain, Campo Cecina
    2000
    C-type print, Diasec
    133 cm x 180 cm

23. MARJAANA KELLA
    Park, Herttoniemi
    2000
    C-type print, Diasec
    133 cm x 180 cm

24. MARJAANA KELLA
    Hypnosis: Harri
    2000
    C-type print, Diasec
    127 cm x 97 cm

25. MARJAANA KELLA
    Hypnosis: Ritva
    C-type print, Diasec
    2000
    127 cm x 97 cm

26. MARJAANA KELLA
    Hypnosis: Raimo No. 3
    2000
    C-type print, Diasec
    127 cm x 97 cm

27. MARJAANA KELLA
    Hypnosis: Ola
    2000
    C-type print, Diasec
    127 cm x 97 cm

28. MARJAANA KELLA
    Hypnosis: Tiina
    2000
    C-type print, Diasec
    127 cm x 97 cm

29. MARJAANA KELLA
    Hypnosis: Marja No. 1
    2000
    C-type print, Diasec
    127 cm x 97 cm

30. MARJAANA KELLA
    Hypnosis: Marja No. 2
    2000
    C-type print, Diasec
    127 cm x 97 cm

31. OLA KOLEHMAINEN
    Institut du Monde Arabe No. 10
    2001
    C-type print, Diasec
    125 cm x 259 cm

32. OLA KOLEHMAINEN
    Institut du Monde Arabe No. 11
    2001
    C-type print, Diasec
    171 cm x 222 cm

List of Works

33. OLA KOLEHMAINEN
Institut du Monde Arabe No. 12
2001
C-type print, Diasec
170 cm x 215 cm

34. OLA KOLEHMAINEN
Institut du Monde Arabe No. 14
2001
C-type print, Diasec
170 cm x 216 cm

35. OLA KOLEHMAINEN
Air
2001
C-type print, Diasec
140 cm x 209 cm

36. ANDREI LAJUNEN
Area Sign A
c. 1997–1998
Portfolio print image: 13.5 cm x 13.5 cm
Overall size of page: 51.5 cm x 41 cm

37. ANDREI LAJUNEN
Policeman
c. 1997–1998
Portfolio print image: 20 cm x 16 cm
Overall size of page: 51.5 cm x 41 cm

38. ANDREI LAJUNEN
Wall
c. 1997–1998
Portfolio print image: 51.5 cm x 41 cm

39. ANDREI LAJUNEN
Policeman
c. 1997–1998
Portfolio print image: 51.5 cm x 41 cm

40. ANDREI LAJUNEN
B Area Sign
c. 1997–1998
Portfolio print image: 33 cm x 33 cm
Overall size of page: 51.5 cm x 41 cm

41. ANDREI LAJUNEN
Stage I
c. 1997–1998
Portfolio print images: 51.5 cm x 41 cm

42. ANDREI LAJUNEN
Stage II–VI
c. 1997–1998
Portfolio print: each panel
13 cm x 13.5 cm
Overall size of page: 51.5 cm x 41 cm

43. ANDREI LAJUNEN
C Area Sign
c. 1997–1998
Portfolio print image: 10.5 cm x 13 cm
Overall size of page: 51.5 cm x 41 cm

44. ANDREI LAJUNEN
Untitled (Skin)
c. 1997–1998
Portfolio print image: 51.5 cm x 41 cm

45. ANDREI LAJUNEN
Hospital Beds
c. 1997–1998
Portfolio print image: 51.5 cm x 41 cm
Portfolio print: each panel
13 cm x 13.5 cm

46. ANDREI LAJUNEN
Untitled (Lion)
c. 1997–1998
Portfolio print image: 34 cm x 33 cm
Overall size of page: 51.5 cm x 41 cm

47. ANDREI LAJUNEN
Untitled (Heliport)
c. 1997–1998
Portfolio print image: 34 cm x 33 cm
Overall size of page: 51.5 cm x 41 cm

48. ANDREI LAJUNEN
Untitled (Police Station I)
c. 1997–1998
Portfolio print image: 51.5 cm x 41 cm

49. ANDREI LAJUNEN
Untitled (Policewoman I)
c. 1997–1998
Portfolio print image: 13.5 cm x 12 cm
Overall size of page: 51.5 cm x 41 cm

50. ANDREI LAJUNEN
Untitled (Policewoman II)
c. 1997–1998
Portfolio print image: 13.5 cm x 12 cm
Overall size of page: 51.5 cm x 41 cm

51. ANDREI LAJUNEN
Untitled (Police Station II)
c. 1997–1998
Portfolio print image: 13.5 cm x 12 cm
Overall size of page: 51.5 cm x 41 cm

52. ANDREI LAJUNEN
Untitled (Graph Paper)
c. 1997–1998
Portfolio print image: 13.5 cm x 12 cm
Overall size of page: 51.5 cm x 41 cm

53. ANDREI LAJUNEN
Hospital Beds
c. 1997–1998
C-type print on aluminium
Diptych, each panel 250 cm x 125 cm

54. ANDREI LAJUNEN
The Wittgenstein Portfolio
c. 1996–1998
Portfolio prints: 11 of varying sizes
Outside measurement of each page is:
51.5 cm x 41 cm

55. JYRKI PARANTAINEN
The Mystery of Satisfaction No. 1
2001
C-type print on aluminium
95 cm x 228 cm

56. JYRKI PARANTAINEN
The Mystery of Satisfaction No. 2
2001
C-type print on aluminium
80 cm x 274 cm

57. JYRKI PARANTAINEN
The Mystery of Satisfaction No. 3
2001
C-type print on aluminium
127 cm x 162 cm

58. JYRKI PARANTAINEN
The Mystery of Satisfaction No. 4
2001
C-type print on aluminium
98 cm x 130 cm

59. JYRKI PARANTAINEN
The Mystery of Satisfaction No. 8
2001
C-type print on aluminium
85 cm x 200 cm